P9-CQX-130

What do you get when you cross a tiger and a parrot?

I don't know, but when it asks for a cracker, you better give it one!

"Doctor," Ms. Luther said to the man, "I think I need glasses."

"I agree," said the man. "This is a bookstore."

What's green and crawls on the ground?

A Girl Scout who dropped her cookies.

What's the easiest way to get from here to there?

Just add the letter "T."

If athletes get athlete's foot, what do astronauts get?

Missile toe.

⊘ SIGNET (0451)

RIB TICKLER/!

☐ **MAD VERTISING, or Up Madison Avenue, An Accumulation of Asinine and Atrocious Advertising Approaches by Dick DeBartolo and Bob Clarke.** You've been duped, taken, swindled, cheated, lied to, conned, and abused by advertising for years! But now, for the *first time*, you are being offered a *real chance* to save money by buying this book (which just might save your life)! (067398—$1.25)

☐ **1,001 GREAT ONE-LINERS by Jeff Rovin.** The greatest one-line jokes, observations, and commentaries, for the first time, put together as a source of information and inspiration for anyone who wants to brighten up a conversation, a speech, or a piece of writing. Instantly prepare and swiftly serve up a feast of laughter. (164229—$3.95)

☐ **1,001 GREAT JOKES by Jeff Rovin.** Over 1,000 jokes, one-liners, riddles, quips and puns—for every audience and every occasion. Among the topics skewered in this collection are: bathrooms, yuppies, hillbillies, sex, small towns, weddings, writers and much more! (168291—$4.95)

☐ **1,001 MORE GREAT JOKES by Jeff Rovin.** Once again we've set a new standard in the wittiest, wackiest, most outrageous in adult humor. Here are jokes for every occasion—from raising chuckles from friends and family, to rousing roars of laughter from all kinds of audiences. Even better, the jokes are organized alphabetically by subject—so open up this book for a nonstop feast of fun from A to Z. (159799—$3.95)

☐ **500 GREAT JEWISH JOKES by Jay Allen.** How did they know Jesus was Jewish? Why did the Jewish mother have her ashes scattered in Bloomingdale's? What's a Jewish porno film? Find out the hilarious answers to these jokes and much more!! (165853—$3.50)

☐ **THE OFFICIAL HANDBOOK OF PRACTICAL JOKES by Peter van der Linden.** A treasury of 144 rib-tickling tricks and leg-pulling pranks. This book will make your eyes water with laughter and the weirdest, wildest, most outrageously inventive and ingenious practical jokes ever assembled. Just make sure that when you read it, no one sees you doing it. Let them all learn about it the right way. The funny way. (158733—$3.50)

Prices slightly higher in Canada

Buy them at your local bookstore or use this convenient coupon for ordering.
NEW AMERICAN LIBRARY
P.O. Box 999, Bergenfield, New Jersey 07621

Please send me the books I have checked above. I am enclosing $_____
(please add $1.00 to this order to cover postage and handling). Send check or money order—no cash or C.O.D.'s. Prices and numbers are subject to change without notice.

Name_____

Address_____

City _____ State _____ Zip Code _____
Allow 4-6 weeks for delivery.
This offer is subject to withdrawal without notice.

500 MORE HILARIOUS JOKES FOR KIDS

BY

JEFF ROVIN

A SIGNET BOOK

SIGNET
Published by the Penguin Group
Penguin Books USA Inc., 375 Hudson Street, New York,
New York 10014, U.S.A.
Penguin Books Ltd, 27 Wrights Lane, London W8 5TZ, England
Penguin Books Australia Ltd, Ringwood, Victoria, Australia
Penguin Books Canada Ltd, 2801 John Street, Markham,
Ontario, Canada L3R 1B4
Penguin Books (N.Z.) Ltd, 182-190 Wairau Road, Auckland 10,
New Zealand

Penguin Books Ltd, Registered Offices: Harmondsworth,
Middlesex, England

First published by Signet, an imprint of New American Library, a
division of Penguin Books USA Inc.

First Printing, September, 1990
10 9 8 7 6 5 4 3 2 1

Copyright © Jeff Rovin, 1990
All rights reserved

 REGISTERED TRADEMARK—MARCA REGISTRADA

Printed in the United States of America

Without limiting the rights under copyright reserved above, no part of
this publication may be reproduced, stored in or introduced into a
retrieval system, or transmitted, in any form, or by any means (electronic,
mechanical, photocopying, recording, or otherwise), without the prior
written permission of both the copyright owner and the above publisher
of this book.

BOOKS ARE AVAILABLE AT QUANTITY DISCOUNTS WHEN USED TO PROMOTE PRODUCTS
OR SERVICES. FOR INFORMATION PLEASE WRITE TO PREMIUM MARKETING DIVISION,
PENGUIN BOOKS USA INC., 375 HUDSON STREET, NEW YORK, NEW YORK 10014.

ACKNOWLEDGMENTS

Special thanks to Adam Heaton, Ryan Quirk, Nate Sheldon, Matt Dunn, Brendan Begnal, and most of all to Sam Rovin.

INTRODUCTION

Here's a question for you: what can be found between soft covers and makes you laugh?

Answer: a clown in your bed!

Another answer, of course, is this book!

What makes *500 More Hilarious Jokes for Kids* so special?

For one thing, it contains many, many jokes you've never heard anywhere. Not only will they give you a chuckle, but you'll have brand-new jokes to tell your friends!

For another thing, the jokes are grouped in topics. If you want to find a joke about a dog or a bug or a pig, just turn to the category of ANIMALS. Or go to SCHOOL and you'll find everything from rotten students to silly teachers. In GHOSTS AND MONSTERS, there are creatures ranging from vampires to zombies to Godzilla and King Kong. Want a gag about football? Baseball? Boxing? Bowling? Take a gander at the chapter on SPORTS.

We've also got KNOCK KNOCK jokes, rib-ticklers about PARENTS, gags about BRATTY

KIDS, and many more. And in the GRAB BAG section, you'll find jokes that didn't fit into the other categories . . . but were just too good to leave out.

For you fans of really disgusto jokes, take a peek at the YUCCH! category, where we introduce the truly sickening Jimmy the Bug-Eater. After reading this section, we promise you'll never even *look* at a worm again.

Here's another question for you: what's black and white and red all over?

Answer: a sunburned penguin. But we also think this book is a good answer, for it's sure to be read over and over!

ANIMALS

Q: Why did the farmer wash the chicken's mouth out with soap?

A. It was using fowl language.

Q. Why do Thanksgiving Turkeys always turn down dessert?

A: They're stuffed.

Q: Why did the farmer name his pig "Ink"?

A: Because it lived in a pen.

Q: What three animals have no trouble getting into locked doors?

A: Don-keys, mon-keys, and tur-keys.

Q: Where do cows go on a date?
A: To the moooovies.

Q: Where do sheep go for a haircut?
A: To the baaa-baaa shop.

Q: How can you tell your new scarecrow is really scary?
A: The crows bring back the corn they stole *last* year!

"I'm so upset," little Margaret said to Dennis. "My dog swallowed a watch."

"What's so bad about that?" Dennis asked.

Margaret replied, "We can't get rid of all the ticks."

Little Jennie wanted a dog, so her mother took her to the pet store. There, Jennie fell in love with a cute little terrier.

"How much is it?" her mother asked the shop owner.

"One hundred dollars."

"Did you raise it?"

"Yes, ma'am," the owner said. "Last week, it was only fifty dollars."

Unfortunately, the day after Jennie bought the dog, it ran away.

Trying to comfort her, Jennie's mother said, "Don't worry, dear. We'll put an ad in the paper with our address and telephone number."

But Jennie just looked at her and said, "Mama, don't be silly! Spot can't read!"

And did you hear about the super-speedy cat that entered the milk-drinking contest? It won by ten laps!

Q: What do you get when you cross a tiger and a parrot?

A: I don't know, but when it asks for a cracker, you better give it one!

Q: How can you tell when an owl is sleeping?
A: It doesn't give a hoot.

Visiting her Uncle Louie on his farm, Samantha agreed to help him with his chores. One morning, he gave her a bucket and told her to get milk from the barn.

"But, Uncle," she said, "I'm afraid I don't know how long cows should be milked."

He replied, "The same as short ones."

Q: What do you get from petting rabbits with sharp teeth?
A: Hare cuts.

Q: How would you describe a frog with broken legs?
A: Unhoppy.

Q: Why is the horse one of the world's most unusual animals?
A: Because it only eats when there isn't a bit in its mouth.

Q: When is it impossible to call the zoo?
A: When the lion is busy.

Q: Why are bulls always in debt?
A: Because they're always charging.

Q: Why are worms so dull?
A: Because everything they do is boring!

Q: Why don't frogs live very long?
A: Because they're always croaking.

Not-very-smart Elliot walked into the pet shop.

"I'd like some birdseed," he said to the clerk.

"Certainly, sir. How many birds do you have?"

"None," said Elliot. "I want to grow some."

Not-very-smart Elliot walked into another pet shop.

"How much are those kittens in the window?" he asked.

"Thirty dollars apiece," said the clerk.

"How much for a whole one?" Elliot asked.

Q: What do you call a boy who sticks his right arm down a lion's throat?

A: Lefty.

Young Alice said to Paula, "Guess why hippos paint their toenails red."

"Why?" asked Paula.

"So they can hide in apple trees."

"Don't be silly!" said Paula. "I've never seen a hippo in an apple tree."

"You see?" said Alice. "It works!"

Q: What did the little boy say when his puppy ran away?

A: "Doggone!"

Q: What's the first step you should take if a lion is about to bite you?
A: A long one.

Charlie said to his kindergarten classmate Joe, "Guess what? Yesterday, I came face-to-face with a ferocious, six-hundred-pound gorilla."

"Really?" said Joe. "Weren't you scared?"

"No. I just walked away from his cage."

Q: What did Mr. Worm say when Worm Jr. came home late?
A: "Where in earth have you been?"

Mrs. Snooty said to Mrs. Humble, "We just sold our prizewinning Great Dane for ten thousand dollars!"

"Big deal," said Mrs. Humble. "*We* just sold our St. Bernard."

"What did you sell it for?" asked Mrs. Snooty.

"Biting the mail carrier," said Mrs. Humble.

Q: What do you get if you cross a hippopota-
mus and a kangaroo?
A: Huge holes all over Australia.

Q: How can you tell which end of a worm is
its head?
A: Tell it a joke, and see which end laughs.

Dr. Griffith and her young assistant were
studying leopards in the jungle.

As they were tiptoeing through the thick
growth, the assistant asked, "Is it difficult to
spot leopards?"

"No," said Dr. Griffith, "they're born that
way."

Q: What would you get if you hooked a rabbit
to your lawn sprinkler?
A: Hare spray.

Q: What kind of cat has eight legs?
A: An octo-puss.

Q: Why did the chicken cross the playground?
A: To get to the other slide.

Q: Why did the cat study medicine?
A: She wanted to become a first-aid kit.

Q: What is gray, has four legs, and a trunk?
A: A mouse taking a vacation.

Q: What was the fate of the frog who parked illegally?
A: It was toad away!

Q: What do you get when you cross a city bird and a frog?
A: We're not sure, but it will probably be pigeon-toad.

Q: Why couldn't Noah play cards on the ark?
A: Hippos were standing on the deck.

Q: What did Noah say when the hippos got off the cards, and he saw how squooshed and tiny they were?
A: "It's no big deal."

Danny said to his friend, "Did you hear about the dog who walked in front of a laser beam and cut off his left side?"

"No!" said the friend. "How's the dog?"

Danny replied, "He's all right."

Danny continued, "I also heard about a duck who got its mouth stuck in a light socket."

"Really? What happened?"

Danny said, "He got an electric bill."

Q: What's the difference between an aquarium and a fast-food restaurant?
A: You can see a man-eating shark in one, and a man eating fries in the other.

Q: What lies on the ground, one hundred feet in the air?
A: A dead centipede.

Q: What do lizards put on their bathroom floors?
A: Rep-tiles.

"Oh no!" cried Mrs. Duck. "I can't find my eggs!"

Mr. Duck tried to calm her down. "Don't worry," he said. "You probably just mis-laid them."

Q: What kind of bedtime stories do baby kangaroos like best?
A: The kind where everyone lives hoppily ever after.

"Please don't bring your dog into the house," Mrs. McGillicutty said to Mrs. Jones. "It's full of fleas."

"I see," said Mrs. Jones. "But you really should have called an exterminator before your house got so bad!"

"You know what they say," said the father and son visiting the zoo. "An elephant never forgets."

"Of course not," said the boy. "What does it have to remember?"

Q: What did the beaver say to the log?
A: "It's been nice gnawing you."

"An elepahnt never forgets," said the father to his son as they visited the zoo.

"Of course not," said the boy. "What does it have to remember?"

While on a photo safari, the tourist said to the guide, "What steps should we take if a lion runs after us?"

The guide answered, "Long ones."

Q: What is a duck's favorite kind of joke?
A: A wise quack.

Q: What do infant insects ride around in?
A: Baby buggies.

Q: Where do you find little, frozen anthills?
A: In Ant-arctica.

"Pssst," Malcolm said to Forbes during a biology test, "how much does a firefly weigh?"

"I don't know," said Forbes, "but they're very light."

"Pssst," Malcolm said to Forbes later in the test, "which is the smartest insect of them all?"

"I don't know," said Forbes, "but the firefly is pretty bright."

"Pssst," said pain-in-the-neck Malcolm, "how do you get fireflies to race?"

"Easy!" Forbes said, "You just shout, 'On your mark, get set—glow!'"

Q: What are the biggest bugs in the world?
A: Gi-ants.

Q: What are the second-biggest bugs in the world?
A: Eleph-ants.

Q: What kind of animal will never sink in water?
A: A gir-raft.

Q: Why did the fly fly?
A: Because the hungry spider spied-her.

The safari guide was very friendly with all the animals, even calling them by pet names. The only thing he feared were the great cats.

One morning, a tourist was startled to see her guide suddenly get up and run from camp.

"Why are you running?" she shouted.

"Dandelion!"

"What? You're afraid of a little flower?"

"Not de flower!" he shouted. "I'm afraid of Fred, Joe, and Dan de lion!"

Q: What part of the body do tics like to bite?
A: Tics attack toes.

Q: What kind of gun do you use to hunt stinging insects?
A: A bee-bee gun, of course!

Q: What kind of insects do really well in school?
A: Spelling bees.

Q: What kind of bugs live at the very bottom of the ocean?
A: Wet ones.

Q: What do you call a newborn bug that lives in a hive?
A: A babe-bee.

Q: What kind of bug has a tough time making up its mind?
A: The may-bee.

Q: What's the difference between a cow with a sore throat and an audience that hates a play?

A: One moos badly, the other boos madly.

Sabu took his pet elephant to the beach.

"Sorry," said the lifeguard, "but we don't allow elephants in the water."

"Why not?" asked Sabu.

"Because they have trouble keeping their trunks up."

Q: Where do you take a sick bunny?

A: To the hops-pital.

Q: What's the best way to teach chickens how to draw?

A: From scratch.

Q: What kind of animal makes the best cheerleader?

A: The zeb-rah!

Q: What kind of dog has to wear glasses?
A: A cock-eyed spaniel.

The woman walked into a pet store.

"Have you got any dogs going cheap?" she asked.

"No, ma'am," said the clerk. "We have birds that go 'cheep.' Our dogs go 'arf.' "

Q: Why don't chickens like addition?
A: Because when they add four and four, they get ate.

Q: What do you get when you cross a chicken with a construction worker?
A: A brick-layer.

Q: What do you get when you cross a big, horned jungle animal with a loaf of bread?
A: A rye-noceros.

Q: What do you get when you plant Lassie in your garden?
A: Collieflower.

Q: How do you keep a skunk from smelling?
A: Put a clothespin on its nose.

Q: What's the difference between a hungry goldfish and a big, fat goldfish?
A: One longs to eat, the other eats too long.

"Don't touch that box!" said the zookeeper to the curious little boy. "I've got a twenty-foot snake in there."

The boy frowned. "Don't give me that baloney! Everyone knows that snakes don't have feet!"

Q: What do you call a lady insect that sucks blood?
A: A Ms. Quito.

When his rooster died, the farmer advertised for a new one. The only rooster who answered the ad came walking in like a big shot, wearing fancy clothes and jewelry, and winking at all the hens.

"I'm afraid I don't like your attitude," said the farmer.

"Why not?" snickered the fowl.

"You're a cocky dude."

"Well," said the bird, "you know what we roosters say? A cocky dude'll do!"

Q: What's a canary's favorite day?
A: It's bird-day.

Q: What do dogs order when they go to the movies?
A: Pupcorn.

The teacher said, "An ocean bird is a seagull, and America's symbol is an eagle. Who can tell me what we call a bird that eats insects?"

Dog-lover Heather replied, "A beegle?"

"Guess what!" Grizelda cried as she ran into the house. "Our cat took first prize at the bird show."

"At the bird show?" said her brother.

"That's right! She took the winner and ate it!"

Q: Why did the lamb run away from home?
A: It wanted to join the fleece circus.

Q: What did the backward roosters crow each morning?
A: "Cock-o-doodle-don't!"

Q: What goes, "Kcauq, Kcauq"?
A: A duck swimming backward.

Q: What's the difference between a dog with a broken leg and a mountain?
A: One's a slow pup, the other a slope up.

Q: Why didn't Farmer Brown put a bell on his cow?
A: He figured that if she got lost, she already had two horns.

Q: What has six legs, two heads, and a tail?
A: A woman on horseback.

Q: What kind of dog doesn't bark, but goes "tick-tock, tick-tock"?
A: A watchdog.

Q: What kind of a hat does a horse wear?
A: A Kentucky Derby, natch!

Q: What kind of dog has the cleanest fur in the world?
A: A shampoodle.

Q: What do you call a science fiction hero who happens to be a water fowl?
A: Duck Rogers.

Q: What's a dog's favorite food?
A: Pawtatoes.

Q: What' a kitten's favorite food?
A: Spag-catti and meowtballs.

Mr. Sousa told Mr. Herbert that his dog Wagner could talk, but Mr. Herbert didn't believe him. So the two men went outside with the animal.

"Now, Mr. Sousa, prove it!" said Mr. Herbert.

Mr. Sousa pointed to the house. "What do we call the flat object on top of the walls, Wagner?"

The dog said, "Roof!"

Mr. Sousa rubbed the bark of a tree. "Is this smooth?"

The dog said, "Rough!"

Mr. Herbert pushed his friend aside. "All

the dog's doing is barking! Let me ask it a question." Bending over Wagner, Mr. Herbert said, "Who is the greatest composer of all time?"

The dog looked at him and said, "Beethoven, though Chopin was best for just the piano."

Mrs. Sousa told Mrs. Herbert that her dog Gilbert could talk. Mrs. Herbert didn't believe her either, so Mrs. Sousa told her to watch.

"Gilbert," she said, "how much is ten minus ten?"

Sure enough, the dog said nothing.

The Sousas also had a rather amazing chicken named Strauss.

"Strauss lays eggs that are a foot long," said Mr. Sousa.

"Incredible," said Mr. Herbert, looking at the egg.

"Not only that, but it talks."

"Really?" said Mrs. Herbert. "What does it say?"

"Ouch."

Q: On the animal baseball team, why was the chicken such a lousy player?

A: Because all the bird could hit were fowl balls.

Q: What position did the kitten play on the team?

A: Cat-cher. (Other animals were already playing meowtfield!)

Q: Who was the team's coach?

A: Yogi Bearra, of course.

Q: Finally, what was the name of the team?

A: The New York Pets. (You should have seen the feathers fly when they played the Baltimore Orioles!)

Q: What did the violin-playing dog do when the audience applauded?

A: She took a bow-wow.

Q: What did the rat say when it saw a bat for the first time?
A: "Look! An angel!"

One day, Mr. Verdi was out walking his pet Spot when Mr. Rossini stopped him.

"That's a mighty unusual-looking dog you have," said the man.

"Unusual, yes. And Spot's the strongest animal in the city."

"Impossible," said Mr. Rossini. "My pit bull is the strongest dog in the city."

In order to find out who was right, the men put the animals together. In less than a minute, Mr. Verdi's pet had knocked the stuffings out of Mr. Rossini's animal.

"Darned if you weren't right!" Mr. Rossini said. "Your Spot is the strongest, no matter how weird he looks!"

"Hmmmm," Mr. Verdi said. "Maybe he wouldn't look so strange if I hadn't cut off his mane."

Q: What's the biggest rodent in the world?
A: A hippopotamouse.

A farmer was driving through the country when he saw the most beautiful German shepherd he'd ever seen. Since he needed a dog to keep foxes from his chicken coop, he stopped by the house and went to the dog's owner.

"Sir—I'll give you one thousand dollars for that dog."

"Sorry," the owner said. "She's not for sale."

"Why not?"

" 'Cause she don't look too good."

"Nonsense," said the man, "she looks fine to me. I'll give you three thousand dollars for her."

The dog's owner accepted the deal, and the man left to put the animal in his car.

A few minutes later, the man came running back.

"Hey!" he screamed. "You sold me a blind dog!"

"Like I told you," said the owner, "she don't look too good!"

Visiting a chicken farm, little Hillary asked the farmer, "Is a chicken old enough to eat when it's a day old?"

"No," smiled the farmer.

"Then how come it doesn't starve?"

The father lion said, "Son, what are you doing?"

"Chasing a hunter, Dad!"

"Well, stop it this instant! I've told you time and time again not to play with your food!"

Q: What do you call a bunch of Australian marsupials?

A: Gang o' roos.

Adam asked June, "Have you ever seen the Catskill Mountains?"

"No," said June, "but I've seen them get rid of mice."

Q: What's the difference between a good friend and a lion's hair?

A: One's a main man, the other's a mane, man.

Q: What do you call a very, very old bug?

A: An ant-ique.

Q: What's the difference between a light snow-fall and a dog getting clipped?
A: One is a wee flurry, the other is a flea worry.

Q: How is a field of grass like a mouse?
A: The cattle eat one, and the cat'll eat the other.

Q: Why do bees born in the spring have trouble making up their minds?
A: Because they're May-bees.

Q: What did the termite say when it saw the burning house?
A: "Mmmmm! I just love a barbeque."

DOCTORS

Mr. Belnick came running in to see Dr. Guest.

"Doctor, you've got to help me! My wife thinks she's a rubber band."

"Tell her to snap out of it!"

Mr. Belnick came running back the next day.

"Doctor, you've got to help me! I keep seeing spots before my eyes!"

"Have you seen an eye doctor?"

"No," Belnick said, "just spots!"

"Doctor," said Hank, "do you think my red, itchy skin will be cured by next week?"

The doctor shrugged. "Now, Hank—you know I hate to make rash promises."

"Well," the man said to his wife, "did the doctor treat you?"

"Treat me, my foot!" she replied. "He charged me fifty dollars!"

"Doctor," said the young woman, "what should I do to have soft hands?"

"Nothing," he replied.

"I'm run-down," said the patient. "What should I do?"

"Get the license number of the car that hit you," said the doctor.

"Please do something for me!" the patient cried to the doctor. "I can't stop thinking that I'm a bridge!"

"What's come over you?" asked the doctor.

"So far, five cars and a truck," said the man.

The patient said to her eye doctor, "Can I bathe with my contact lenses?"

"You can," said the doctor, "but I think a washcloth would work much better."

"I have good news and bad news," the doctor told his patient.

"What's the bad news?"

"You've caught a disease that only birds usually get."

"Oh my!"

"But don't worry," said the doctor. "It can be tweeted."

"Doctor!" the man screamed into the phone. "You've got to help me. I know a woman who thinks she's an owl!"

"Who?"

"Oh no!" the man yelled. "Not you too!"

"You've got to help me, doc," pleaded Mr. Horowitz. "I just swallowed my harmonica!"

"You should be glad," said the doctor.

"Be glad? About what?"
"That you don't play the piano!"

Q: Why did the dentist never fix the teeth of
people with glasses?
A: Because he felt that a drill worked better.

"Doctor," the patient cried, "I've only got
sixty seconds to live!"
"Wait a minute, please. . . ."

"Doctor," the patient moaned, "I keep thinking I'm a piano!"
"Wait, while I make some notes. . . ."

"Doctor," the patient wailed, "you've taken
out my appendix and my tonsils, but I still
don't feel well!"
"Look, I've had enough out of you. . . ."

"Doctor," the patient complained, "I can't stop thinking that I'm a brick wall!"

"Don't worry, you'll get over it."

After Mr. Murrow had a tooth pulled, he went to pay the bill.

"Four hundred dollars!" he yelled. "That's outrageous! I thought it was only supposed to be one hundred dollars!"

"It was," said the receptionist. "But you screamed so loudly that three other patients ran away!"

After being knocked out by a falling brick, a woman awoke in a hospital.

Her head was killing her, and she said weakly, "Was I brought here . . . to die?"

"Actually, no," said the doctor. "You were brought here yesterday."

Mr. Rhodes had a badly swollen nose, and went to see the doctor.

"How did you get that?" the doctor asked.

"I was out in the garden and bent down to sniff a brose."

"There's no 'b' in 'rose,' " said the doctor.

"There was in this one," replied Mr. Rhodes.

Q: What do you call a dentist who's good at adding or taking away teeth?

A: A mouthematician.

"Doctor!" screamed the boy. "My sister just fell down a flight of stairs!"

"Cellar?" asked the doctor.

"No. Who'd buy her with two broken legs?"

"It's the latest thing," said the doctor to his patient. "A pill that has a painkiller and glue."

"What's it do?" asked the patient.

"It cures a splitting headache."

"Doctor," said Arthur, "I just swallowed a peach pit!"

"Are you choking?"

"No! I'm *serious*!"

The dentist said, "In order to get rid of your toothache, I'll need a drill."

The surprised patient said, "You mean, you can't fix a tooth without a rehearsal?"

"How's the stomachache?" Dr. Klein asked Mrs. Hager.

"Not bad, thanks."

"Have you been drinking warm milk after a hot bath, like I told you?"

"I have," Mrs. Hager said, "though it's tough to get the milk down after drinking the bath."

"Do you know how many famous surgeons were born in New York?" one doctor asked another.

"How many?"

"None. Just babies."

"Doctor, can you help me out?" the patient cried.

"Certainly. You just go through the same door you used to come in."

Q: Why did the doctor give up practicing medicine?
A: She had no patients.

Mr. Queeg said to the psychiatrist, "Doctor, you've got to cure me! I can't stop thinking that I'm a ladder."

"Of course I'll cure you," the doctor said. "We'll just have to take one step at a time."

"Doctor," Ms. Luthor said to the man, "I think I need glasses."

"I agree," said the man. "This is a bookstore."

Q: What did the doctor say when he was walking down the street and saw a herd of dinosaurs rushing toward him?

A: "Uh-oh. I think I'm in the wrong joke!"

Q: What are a dentist's least favorite letters?

A: D-K.

GRAB BAG

The barber was giving Mr. Burma a shave.

"Tell me," said the barber, "are you wearing a red tie?"

"No, I'm not."

"In that case," said the barber, "I'm afraid I've just slit your throat!"

Lovesick Lonnie said to Bonnie, "One day, my dearest, would you be my wife?"

Bonnie snorted, "One day? I wouldn't be your wife for one minute!"

Q: What goes dot-dash-brrrr, dot-dot-brrrr?
A: Someone communicating in Morse Cold.

Clark said to his friend, "My fiancée keeps telling her friends she's marrying the handsomest man in the world."

"That's too bad," said the friend. "I thought she was going to marry you."

Two comedy-club owners were chatting.

"Last week," said one, "we had the most incredible young man I've ever seen. He did the best animal impressions in the world. Unfortunately, we had to fire him."

"If he was so good, why did you fire him?"

"Because he didn't do animal sounds. He did the smells."

Q: What's the last thing you take off before going to bed?

A: Your feet, from the floor.

"Well," the builder said to his young apprentice, "you're really hammering in those nails like lightning."

"I'm pretty fast, huh, boss?"

"No," said the builder. "I meant you never strike the same place twice."

Q: What's the difference between a dog groomer and an iceberg?
A: One brushes coats, the other crushes boats.

Q: What's green and crawls on the ground?
A: A girl scout who dropped her cookies.

Q: What gets wetter as it dries?
A: A towel.

Grandpa Roy said to Randy, "A dime and a nickel were sitting on a wall. The nickel fell off; why didn't the dime?"

"That's easy," said Randy. "The dime had more cents."

Q: What's white and rises?
A: A dumb snowflake.

Q: Why do churchgoers say "Amen" instead of "Awomen"?
A: Because they sing hymns, not hers.

Billy-Sol said to Big Jim, "I'll have you know, I have royal blood in my veins."

"Whose?" said Big Jim. "King Kong's?"

Clumsy Jackson walked into the paint store and asked the clerk, "Do you have any wallpaper I can put on myself?"

"No," said the clerk. "We only have wallpaper you can put on walls."

Jodi asked her friend, "Did you hear the joke about the rope?"

"No. Tell me."

"Aw . . . just skip it."

Little Sheppy came running into the house, tears running down his cheeks.

"Ma! That idiot Mike bit my leg at school!"

"How awful!" his mother cried. "Did you put anything on it?"

"No," Sheppy replied. "He like it just the way it was."

Q: Where would you go to buy an ax?
A: A chopping mall.

Q: Why are traffic lights always turning red?
A: Because they're forced to change in the middle of the street.

Out in the Wild West, a cowboy came upon an Indian frantically sending smoke signals.

"What's wrong?" asked the cowboy.

"We haven't had water for nearly two weeks."

"I see. And you're sending a message to the gods?"

"No," said the Indian. "I'm calling for a plumber."

Q: Are most houses built with a stoop?
A: No. Most of them are built straight.

Q: What's the best way to carve wood?
A: Whittle by whittle.

Q: Why did the workers at the government mint go on strike?
A: They wanted to make less money.

"This is terrible!" said one peasant to another. "I hear the dictator is going to charge us money every time we use our thumbs."

"That *is* horrible!"

"And if we don't pay, he's going to kill us!"

"We must revolt," said the other peasant. "After all, who ever heard of using thumb tax to hang people?"

Sid asked Mr. Dithers, "Did you hear the story about the broken pencil?"

"No. It sounds dumb."

"It *is* dumb," said Sid. "It has no point at all!"

The mail carrier walked up to the man watering his lawn.

"Is this magazine for you?" the postal worker asked. "I can't tell, the name is torn."

"Then it can't be mine," said the man. "My name isn't Torn."

Felix said to Oscar, "Did you hear the joke about the letter with no postage?"

"No."

"Never mind. You wouldn't get it.

Q: What runs around a yard without moving an inch?

A: A fence.

Q: What travels around the world without ever leaving its corner?
A: A postage stamp.

Q: How did the barber clip more heads than any other barber in town?
A: He took short cuts.

Q: Why is the letter "Y" so important to a lady?
A: Without it, she'd be a lad.

Q: Why was the tiny island called "T?"
A: Because it was in the middle of water.

Q: How long ago were there only three vowels in the alphabet?
A: Years ago . . . before "U" and "I" were born!

Q: How did Lucy get lucky?
A: She found a "K."

Q: Estelle graduated from college and became a doctor, changed her mind and became a writer, then changed her mind again and became a doctor until she died. What would you call her?
A: Dead.

Q: What can be held without ever being touched?
A: A conversation.

Q: What can everyone draw, even if they're not an artist?
A: Breath.

Q: How can you tell Los Angeles air is too smoggy?
A: The birds wake up coughing.

Q: What kind of table has no legs?
A: A multiplication table.

Q: Where can you always find money, fame, and power?
A: In the dictionary.

HISTORY

Q: Why did George Washington go down in history?

A: He forgot to do his homework.

Q: What kind of music did the Pilgrims enjoy?

A: Plymouth Rock.

Q: Why are so many Pilgrims buried in Massachusetts?

A: Because they're dead.

Q: When the Pilgrims reached the New World, where exactly did they stand?

A: On their feet.

Q: Where was the Declaration of Independence signed?

A: At the bottom, of course.

Q: Why are medieval times also known as the "Dark Ages?"

A: Because there were so many knights.

Q: What did Adam say on the last day of the year?

A: "It's almost New Year's, Eve."

Adam was also the fastest runner in history. After all, he was first in the human race!

As for the saddest person in history, that had to be the giant Goliath. He was famous for his great sighs.

Q: If George Washington was the father of his country, what does that make his pet chicken Ralph?

A: The feather of his country.

Davy Crockett and Jim Bowie were walking through the woods.

"Have you ever hunted bear?" Davy asked.

"No," said Bowie. "I always put my clothes on."

Q: How was Moses able to part the Red Sea?

A: He used a sea-saw.

Q: Why did the Indian wear feathers on his head?

A: To keep his wig-wam.

Q: Which Indian was in charge of facial tissues?

A: The hankie-chief.

Q: Where did Indians like to drink hot beverages?
A: In a tea-pee.

Q: Which American president was once a farmer?
A: George Bushel.

Q: Which American president is fond of fishing?
A: Jimmy Cod-er.

Q: In what battle was Colonel William Travis killed?
A: His last one.

Q: Where was King Solomon's Temple?
A: On the side of his head.

In the Old West, Robber Jesse went to check on Robber Frank, who was waiting for the stagecoach to come through. Frank's ear was still pressed against the ground.

"Any signs of the stagecoach?"

"Yes. It came through an hour ago."

"An hour ago! How can you tell?"

Frank answered, "It ran over my neck."

Q: Who wanted to conquer the world, but was still very, very sweet?

A: Attila the Honey.

Q: Where did Mark Twain live?

A: At a wailwoad station.

One ancient Roman said to the other, "Do you know why eleven o'clock at night is very important to the wife of our ruler?"

"Yes," said the other. "That's when Julius sees her."

Q: What is the difference between an historical scholar and someone who drives a getaway car?

A: One cracks books, the other backs crooks.

INSULTS

When you start to sing, people clap their hands—right over their ears!

Musicians run in your family. They have to run, before people stone them.

Can I drop you off on the way home? Say—off the roof?

Things could be worse. There could be two of you.

I don't know what I'd do without you . . . but I enjoy thinking about it!

You're handsome, in a way—very far away.

There're only two things wrong with you. Everything you do, and everything you say.

I never forget a face, but in your case I'll make an exception.

You deserve a big hand . . . right across your backside.

I love your new outfit! Is it Halloween already?

You know, those clothes fit you like a glove. A baseball glove.

I could tell people wonderful things about you, but I only tell the truth.

You're such a rat that if you threw a boomerang, it wouldn't come back.

The only way to expand your mind is to put gunpowder in your ears and light it.

Tell me everything you know. I have a few seconds to kill.

The only exercise you ever get is pushing your luck.

In fact, you're such a wimp you couldn't even crack a joke . . . or lick a postage stamp!

Most people have brainstorms. You only have a drizzle.

Don't ever give anyone a piece of your mind. You can't afford to lose it.

You had a terrible accident in your early youth: you were born.

You're so stupid, you failed lunch period.

I've really enjoyed our chat. My brain needed a rest.

You have the face of a saint . . . a Saint Bernard.

Would you help make our neighborhood more beautiful? Move.

You're so cheap, you won't even pay attention!

You're a real treasure. In fact, someone ought to bury you.

You're related to a Boone, huh? Which one: Daniel Boone or a baboon?

It's okay if you let your mind wander. It's too weak to go anywhere.

Sure I'm listening to you. Can't you tell I'm falling asleep?

You're like a Snickers bar without the chocolate: just nuts.

Everyone says you're a stupid pig, but I don't think you're a pig.

I know what's on your mind: a germ. It's the only thing that could fit.

KNOCK-KNOCKS

Knock, knock
Who's there?
Santa.
Santa who?
Santa letter and tell me what you want for Christmas.

Knock, knock.
Who's there?
Owen.
Owen who?
Owen to see you, so open up!

Knock, knock.
Who's there?
Annie.
Annie who?
Anniebody gonna let me in?

Knock, knock.
Who's there?
Manuel.
Manuel who?
Manuel be sorry if you don't unlock the door!

Knock, knock.
Who's there?
Ice cream.
Ice cream who?
Ice cream when I hurt myself!

Knock, knock.
Who's there?
Justin.
Justin who?
Justin case I don't see you, have a nice trip!

Knock, knock.
Who's there?
Isabel.
Isabel who?
Isabel louder than a knock?

Knock, knock.
Who's there?
Ya.
Ya, who?
Well, I didn't think you'd be so happy to see me!

Knock, knock.
Who's there?
Abbie.
Abbie who?
Abbie birthday to you.

Knock, knock.
Who's there?
Dewey.
Dewey who?
Dewey have to wipe our feet before we come in?

Knock, knock.
Who's there?
Candy.
Candy who?
Candy-magine why you're not letting me in!

Knock, knock.
Who's there?
Ivan.
Ivan who?
Ivan hour to visit, so open the door!

Knock, knock.
Who's there?
Howl.
Howl who?
Howl you know when an hour's up?

Knock, knock.
Who's there?
Juan.
Juan who?
Juan to come out and play?

Knock, knock.
Who's there?
Ooze.
Ooze who?
Ooze gonna let me in?

Knock, knock.
Who's there?
Betty.
Betty who?
Betty you thought I was going to be late.

Knock, knock.
Who's there?
Police.
Police who?
Police let me in, it's freezing!

Knock, knock.
Who's there?
Rita.
Rita who?
Rita book instead of watching so much TV!

Knock, knock.
Who's there?
Sawyer.
Sawyer who?
Sawyer car in the driveway, so I decided to stop by.

Knock, knock.
Who's there?
Tennis.
Tennis who?
Tennis what you get by adding five plus five.

Knock, knock.
Who's there?
Doris.
Doris who?
Doris open, mind if I come in?

Knock, knock.
Who's there?
Hugo.
Hugo who?
Hugo walk the dog, it's freezing!

Knock, knock.
Who's there?
Mr. Hyde.
Mr. Hyde who?
Mister, Hyde like to come in!

Knock, knock.
Who's there?
Francis.
Francis who?
Francis where they speak French.

Knock, knock.
Who's there?
Sarah.
Sarah who?
Sarah chair around here? I'm tired of standing.

Knock, knock.
Who's there?
Watson.
Watson who?
Watson who with you? There's nothing new with me!

Knock, knock.
Who's there?
Mary.
Mary who?
Marry you? I hardly *know* you.

Knock, knock.
Who's there?
Willie.
Willie who?
Willie you come out and play with me?

Knock, knock.
Who's there?
Felix.
Felix who?
Felix-tremely chilly . . . let me in!

Knock, knock.
Who's there?
Carol.
Carol who?
Carol go if you step on the gas.

Knock, knock.
Who's there?
Michael.
Michael who?
Mike'll smash the door down if you don't open up!

Knock, knock.
Who's there?
Emma.
Emma who?
Emma your new neighbor. I just came by to say hi.

Knock, knock.
Who's there?
Barbara.
Barbara who?
Barbara black sheep, have you any wool . . .?

Knock, knock.
Who's there?
Olive.
Olive who?
Olive in this house. What are you doing here?

Knock, knock.
Who's there?
Alex.
Alex who?
Alex plain why I'm here if you let me in.

Knock, knock.
Who's there?
Phyllis.
Phyllis who?
Phillis bag with candy, it's Trick or Treat.

Knock, knock.
Who's there?
Luke.
Luke who?
Luke outside and you'll see!

Knock, knock.
Who's there?
Kermit.
Kermit who?
Kermit a crime and you'll go to jail.

Knock, knock.
Who's there?
House.
House who?
House soon will you be ready to leave?

Knock, knock.
Who's there?
Just a ghost.
Just a ghost who?
Just a ghost to show you, I'm never late.

Knock, knock.
Who's there?
Waiter.
Waiter who?
Waiter minute, I'll be right in.

Knock, knock.
Who's there?
Lettuce.
Lettuce who?
Lettuce in, it's raining!

Knock, knock.
Who's there?
Alison.
Alison who?
Alison to records with you, if you open the door.

Knock, knock.
Who's there?
Arthur.
Arthur who?
Arthur any Trick or Treat candies left?

Knock, knock.
Who's there?
Donkey.
Donkey who?
Donkey you very much for answering the door.

Knock, knock.
Who's there?
Wendy.
Wendy who?
Wendy door is open, I'll come in.

Knock, knock.
Who's there?
Major.
Major who?
Major open the door, didn't I?

Knock, knock.
Who's there?
Europe.
Europe who?
Europe early today, aren't you?

Knock, knock.
Who's there?
Arthur.
Arthur who?
Arthur any other people living here?

Knock, knock.
Who's there?
Juno.
Juno who?
Juno what time it is? I forgot my watch.

Knock, knock.
Who's there?
Ken.
Ken who?
Ken I please come in?

Knock, knock.
Who's there?
Owl.
Owl who?
Ow'll you know if you don't open up?

Knock, knock.
Who's there?
Noah.
Noah who?
Noah good place we can go for dinner?

Knock, knock.
Who's there?
Howard.
Howard who?
Howard you like to stand out here while some-
one asks, "Who's there?"

Knock, knock.
Who's there?
Olaf.
Olaf who?
Olaf, and I'll puff, and I'll blow your door
down!

Knock, knock.
Who's there?
Diplomas.
Diplomas who?
Diploma's here to fix your leaking sink.

Knock, knock.
Who's there?
Jewel.
Jewel who?
Jewel be happy to see who it is at the door.

Knock, knock.
Who's there?
Chester.
Chester who?
Chester minute! Don't you know who this is?

Knock, knock.
Who's there?
Snow.
Snow who?
Snow use! I can't open the door.

Knock, knock.
Who's there?
Hugh.
Hugh who?
Yoo-hoo to you, too!

Knock, knock.
Who's there?
Detail.
Detail who?
Detail-ophone repair person.

Knock, knock.
Who's there?
Amanda.
Amanda who?
Amanda fix the washer!

Knock, knock.
Who's there?
Dawn.
Dawn who?
Dawn you leave me standing in the cold!

Knock, knock.
Who's there?
Fanny.
Fanny who?
Fanny body calls, I'll be at the bowling alley.

Knock, knock.
Who's there?
I'm Gladys.
I'm Gladys who?
I'm Gladys see you!

Knock, knock.
Who's there?
Jackson.
Jackson who?
Jack's on the telephone, so I thought I'd come over.

Knock, knock.
Who's there?
Juliet.
Juliet who?
Juliet like a pig, but she's feeling better now.

Knock, knock.
Who's there?
Mandy.
Mandy who?
Mandy battle stations! Here comes the enemy!

Knock, knock.
Who's there?
Patty.
Patty who?
Patty dog on the head, and it won't bite you.

Knock, knock.
Who's there?
Paul.
Paul who?
Paul hard! I can't open the door.

Knock, knock.
Who's there?
N Vitamin.
N Vitamin who?
N Vitamin, or he'll stand outside all day!

Knock, knock.
Who's there?
Alvin.
Alvin who?
Alvin the lottery if you lend me some money.

MUSIC

After a steamroller went out of control and rolled through a ranch, the rancher looked at all his squashed cattle and said to a hired hand, "Well, at least we still have music."

"Music?" said the hand, scratching his head. "I don't hear any music."

"Look around! Can't you see the beef-flat?"

Q: What does a piano bench with a broken leg think of pianists?
A: It just can't bear them.

Q: What kind of scientists love music the most?
A: Geologists. They dig rock.

Q: What do you call a tuba's father?
A: Oom-papa.

"Myron plays entirely by ear," said the proud parents as the little boy hammered away at the piano.

A visitor complained, "Too bad we all have to listen that way, too."

Q: Who's a dog's favorite composer?
A: Wag-ner.

Q: Who is the most dangerous composer to punch?
A: The one who will hit you Bach.

"Mom," said Arnold, the young violinist, "it's time for me to go and give my recital."

"What!" screamed the mother. "With holes in your trousers?"

"No," he said, "with my violin."

Q: What song is a favorite among the
   Eskimos?
A: "Freeze a Jolly Good Fellow."

Q: Who wrote that Eskimo favorite?
A: Mozarctic.

Al said to his playmate, "You know, my
trumpet is the best present I ever got."
   "Really? I never even heard you play it."
   "Exactly," said Al. "My mom gives me a
dollar a week *not* to play it!"

Q: What did Mr. Krupa say when his son
   came into the bedroom pounding on his
   drums?
A: "Beat it!"

In England, Mrs. Bentley was thrilled when her husband called and said that he had two tickets for an American plane and was coming home to get her.

Mrs. Bentley had never been to America, and quickly packing her bags, she threw them in the trunk of the car and drove to the train station to meet her husband. When he arrived, he got behind the wheel. Much to Mrs. Bentley's surprise, the car pulled to a stop at a concert hall.

"What are we doing here?" she asked with horror.

Mr. Bentley replied, "Why, my dear, we've come to hear the American playin'."

Q: What did Mrs. Williams say when her son decided to take up the guitar?
A: "Why pick that?"

The Noodlemans went to the pianist's concert and were extremely bored.

"For my next selection," said the musician, "I will play 'Over the Rainbow.' "

"Thank goodness," said Mrs. Noodleman to her husband. "I thought he was going to stay all night!"

Mr. Viafore was singing in the shower when there was a knock at the front door. When he opened it, he found a woman standing outside.

"I'm Mrs. Thorne, the singing teacher."

"But I didn't call for a singing teacher."

"I know," said Mrs. Thorne. "Your neighbors did."

But Mr. Viafore kept on singing on the shower. The next day, there was another knock at the door. This time, it was one of the neighbors.

"Say," said the neighbor, "do you know 'The Beautiful Blue Danube?' "

"As a matter of fact I do," said Mr. Viafore proudly.

"Good. Then go and jump in it!"

After helping him through a very difficult piece, the music teacher turned to her pupil.

"Now, Sean, do you have any questions?"

"Just one, ma'am."

"Very well. What is it?"

Sean asked, "When's the lesson over?"

Mrs. Feinson stopped to watch her son's heavy-metal rock group rehearsing in the garage.

"I think you should be on TV," Mrs. Feinson said.

"Really, Mom? We're that good?"

"I don't know," she said, "but at least then I could turn the sound off."

"So, professor," said the proud mother. "Do you think my Linda should take up the violin as a career?"

"No," said the professor, "I think she should put it down as an act of kindness."

Passing by the unusual store, Peter went inside.

"I notice that you only sell drums and shotguns," he said to the owner. "Isn't that a very unusual combination?"

"Not at all," said the owner. "We find that if someone buys drums one day, then their neighbor comes in and buys a shotgun the next day."

"Don't you think my singing is out of this world?" the young music student asked her friend.

"Yes," said her friend. "In fact, you should try doing it on the moon."

After the concert, the terrible singer walked over to the manager of the music hall.

"Did you notice," said the singer, "how my magnificent voice filled the room?"

"Yes," said the manager. "In fact, I saw people leaving to make room for it."

Q: What's the easiest dance in the world to learn?
A: The Elevator. There are no steps.

"Say, Jean," said Pierre, "did you hear that there's a new kind of piano? It's got a fan built right into the keyboard."

"Why?" asked Jean.

"It's for people who like to play it cool."

Q: What's the best way to clean an orchestra's horn section?
A: With a tuba toothpaste.

It was young Terrence's first time at a concert.

"What are those pages the musicians keep looking at?" he asked his father.

"That's the musical score."

Terrence said, "I didn't know the musicians get points for playing!"

Q: What do you call the person who answers the telephone at the Metropolitan Opera House?
A: An opera-tor.

Q: Why is the snake such a musical animal?
A: Because of all its scales.

Q: What do you call people who only pretend to be composers?
A: Sym-phonies.

Q: What's a rock singer's favorite snack food?
A: Elvis Pretzel.

Q: Which composer spent a lot of time fishing?
A: Bait-hoven.

Q: What's the difference between a popular gelatin desert and President Ford's string instrument?
A: One is cherry Jell-O, the other is Jerry's cello.

Q: What do you call a band of angels that plays headbanger music?
A: Heaven metal musicians.

The orchestra leader was embarrassed by the rowdy behavior of his musicians. He tapped his baton on the music stand for attention.

"I'm ashamed of you!" he said. "Throwing music at each other and shouting like that! What's wrong with you?"

"Maestro," said one of the musicians, "if we knew how to conduct ourselves, we wouldn't need you."

OUTER SPACE

Q: Why is the letter "T" so powerful?
A: Because it makes a star start.

Q: Why did the moon refuse to have dessert?
A: It was full.

Q: What keeps the moon from falling out of the sky?
A: Moonbeams, naturally!

Q: If athletes get athlete's foot, what to astronauts get?
A: Missile toe.

Q: Where do space shuttle pilots keep their meals?
A: In launch boxes.

Q: What kind of food do Martian squirrels eat?
A: Astro-nuts.

Q: What do you call a planet after it's five billion years old?
A: Five billion and one.

The long, square robot from Mars landed in Chicago and saw a man carrying a boom box. Furious, the robot ran over and yelled, "Your child is crying, sir! Why don't you feed it?"

Q: What's white, round, and crazy?
A: A fool moon.

Q: What's the difference between parade musicians and a four-eyed creature who's told to get off the Red Planet and never return?

A: One's a marching band, the other's a Martian banned.

Q: What do they call the most important tennis match on Mars?

A: The UFOpen.

Q: What do you use to propel a ship around the Milky Way?

A: Mete-oars.

Q: How do astronauts see in the dark reaches of outer space?

A: They turn on satel-lights.

"You've got to help me," the astronaut said to the doctor. "I've turned chicken! I simply can't leave the earth again!"

"Well," the doctor replied, "I'm afraid there's no cure for what you have."

"What *do* I have?"

The doctor replied, "Atmos-fear."

Q: What moves through space quicker than an asteroid?
A: A fasteroid.

Q: What do you call a car that can be driven on the moon?
A: An astron-auto.

SCHOOL

"Jason," said the teacher, "can you tell me what Attila the Hun's middle name was?"

After thinking for a moment, the young student replied, "The?"

Mr. Kaplan, the science teacher, asked Paula, "Can you tell me what a pteranodon is?"

Nodding confidently, Paula said, "A UFO."

Mr. Kaplan said, "I'm sorry, but that's wrong. It's a winged, prehistoric animal."

"Exactly," said Paula. "It's a flying 'saur, sir."

Finding out what her new students knew about the Bible, the Sunday-school teacher pointed to a young boy and said, "Billy, can you tell me who built the ark?"

Shifting in his seat, Billy said, "No . . . uh . . ."

Smiling, the teacher said, "That's right."

The nursery-school teacher walked to little Barbara.

"What are you doing?" the teacher asked.

"Writing a letter to my little brother," she said.

"That's very sweet," said the teacher, "but you don't know how to write."

"That's okay," said Barbara. "My brother doesn't know how to read, either."

Q: What word is always pronounced incorrectly, even by the smartest people on earth?

A: Incorrectly.

"Can someone tell me," asked the fifth-grade math teacher, "how you would divide thirteen potatoes equally among seven people?"

"Sure," said Harold. "You mash 'em."

The fifth-grade science teacher didn't have much better luck with her class.

"Who can explain why the nose is in the middle of your face?" she asked.

Harold raised his hand again. "Because it's always the scenter," he said.

Still determined to teach her class something, the science teacher asked, "Which of the senses is hurt the most when you're sick?"

Harold's hand shot up. "Your sense of touch," he said.

"Touch? What makes you say that?"

"Because," said Harold, "when you're sick, you don't feel well."

But the science teacher didn't give up. While showing the students an experiment involving chemicals, she asked for a volunteer to help mix them.

Harold raised his hand.

"Do you think you're responsible?" the teacher asked.

"No doubt about it," said Harold. "Every time something happens in my house, my mom always says I'm responsible!"

Still wanting to teach Harold something, the science teacher said, "What name do we give a star with a tail?"

Bright Suzy raised her hand. "A comet," she said.

"Baloney," said Harold. "A star with a tail is Benji."

Desperate to educate Harold, the science teacher asked, "Which do you think burns longer? Candles made from fat, or candles made from wax?"

"Neither," said Harold. "They both burn shorter."

The geography teacher also ended up tearing out his hair.

"In what country is Boston located?" he asked the class.

"France," Harold said at once.

"Don't be ridiculous," said the teacher. "What part of Boston is in France?"

Harold replied, "The letter 'n.' "

Harold's English teacher also had her problems with the boy.

"Who can use the word 'toast' in a sentence?"

"I can," Harold said, and cleared his throat. "I eated four pieces of toast for breakfast."

The teacher gently corrected him. "You mean ate, Harold."

"Eight?" he said. "What do you think I am, a pig?"

Needless to say, Harold's history teacher had his hands full.

"You know, class," he said, "at your age, George Washington wasn't just listening to music and playing. He was already a bold courier for the army!"

"And at your age," Harold said, "he wasn't teaching in a crummy school, he was President of the United States!"

Finally, Harold's sister Henrietta gave her home-economics teacher some problems.

"Are you finished filling the saltshakers?" the woman asked the girl.

"No," said Henrietta. "Y'know, it isn't easy putting the salt into these tiny holes!"

"So," Aunt Rose said to her young nephew Paulie, "how do you like school?"

"Closed," said the boy.

Q: What is the only question which you must always answer with a "no"?
A: What does "n-o" spell?

"Boy," young Mikey said to his mother when he came home from school, "our teacher is really a dummie!"

"How can you say that?" the shocked mother asked.

"Well, yesterday she asked us how much one plus one is, and we told her. But she still doesn't know the answer. Today, she asked us again!"

"Class," said the teacher, "can anyone tell me if there's a single word which contains every vowel?"

One boy said, "Unquestionably—but I can't think of what it is."

"Marcie," said the teacher, "how do you spell 'library?' "

"L-I-B-E-R-R-Y."

"No," said the teacher, "that's not right."

"Sure it is!" said Marcie. "You asked me how *I* spell it. Well, that's how I spell it!"

"Now, children," said the teacher to her first-graders, "who can tell me how many letters there are in the alphabet."

After thinking for a moment, Lucille raised her hand. "Eleven!" said the girl.

"I'm sorry," said the teacher, "but that isn't right."

"It sure is," said the girl. "T-h-e a-l-p-h-a-b-e-t."

Lucille's teacher smiled and said, "That's very funny. But how many letters are there in the alphabet—from a to z?"

Again, Lucille raised her hand. "There are twenty-six letters," she said, "except on Christmas, when there are only twenty-five."

"Why only twenty-five?" asked the teacher.

Lucille said, "Because on Christmas, everyone says 'no-el.'"

Ignoring Lucille, the teacher continued her English lesson.

"Class," she said, "what letter does it take the longest to reach?"

Lucille answered, "It's 'H!' "

"No," said the patient teacher, "the answer is 'Z.' "

"It can't be," said Lucille. " 'H' is at the end of the earth."

Q: What did the sign say outside the karate class?
A: "Please don't knock before entering."

"If Abraham Lincoln were alive today," said the teacher, "what would he find that he was most famous for?"

Ricky raised his hand and answered, "Old age."

Q: What's dirty when its white, and clean when it's black?
A: A blackboard.

"Did you know," said the teacher, "that it takes at least six sheep to make a sweater?"

"Really?" said dull Dennis. "I didn't even know they could knit!"

"Can anyone tell me what makes the Tower of Pisa lean?" Mrs. Heininger asked her class.

"I can," said Sam. "It doesn't eat much!"

When clumsy Hector brought home his report card, his father asked, "What marks did you get in gym?"

"I didn't get any marks," said Hector. "Just a lot of bruises."

The teacher said, "Who can tell me the name of Egypt's largest river?"

Rebecca said, "The Nile."

"Correct. And can you tell me the name of some of Egypt's smaller rivers?"

Rebecca thought, then said, "The Juve-Niles?"

The science teacher asked, "What's the biggest change that takes place when water turns to ice?"

Practical Patty answered, "The store charges you more for it."

"Ronnie," said the teacher, "spell 'missile.' "

"Sure. M-i-s-s-s-i-l-e."

"Almost. Leave out an 's.' "

"Okay," said Ronnie. "Which one?"

The English teacher asked, "Who can tell me the name of the poet that wrote, 'To a Field Mouse?' "

"I don't know," said Gus, "but I'd like to know if the field mouse wrote back."

The teacher held up a test paper.

"Messy Marvin," she said, "is this yours? The name is smudged."

"It can't be," Marvin said. "My last name is Smith."

"Paul Bunyan was so tall," said the teacher, "that his bed was over fifty feet long!"

Doubting Thomas said, "That sounds like a lot of bunk to me!"

"Who can name five sea animals?" asked the teacher.

"I can," said Dale. "Four whales and a dolphin."

"I hate my new teacher!" Bertha said to Diana.

"Why?"

"Because she told me to change seats for the present . . . and then she never gave me one!"

The art teacher looked at Sally's painting, which was all brown on the bottom and all blue on top.

"That's very interesting," said the teacher. "What's it supposed to be?"

"A cow grazing in the field."

"I see. Where's the grass?"

"The cow ate it all."

"But then, where's the cow?"

"You don't think it would be dumb enough to stick around after eating all the grass, do you?"

"Wally," said the teacher, "you missed school yesterday."

"No, I didn't!"

"Don't tell me you didn't," the teacher snapped. "You weren't here."

"You're right," said Wally, "I wasn't here. But I didn't miss it one bit!"

"Tammy," said the teacher, "name two pronouns."

The nervous girl stuttered, "Who . . . me?"

"That's right," the teacher smiled.

"Who can recite Lincoln's Gettysburg Address?" asked the history teacher.

"I can," said Greg. "It was the White House, Washington, D.C."

The art teacher looked over her student's shoulder. "That's a very nice drawing of a stagecoach, Bruce, but there are no wheels. What holds it up?"

"Bandits," he said.

"Who can tell me where hippos are found?" asked the teacher.

Bernice said, "Teacher, don't be silly! They're so big they never get lost."

While waiting for the bus, Crystal said to Lisa, "My brother beats me up every single morning."

"That's terrible!" Lisa said.

"I know. He gets up at six, but I don't get out of bed until six-thirty."

"Peter," snapped the teacher, "I wish you'd pay a little attention!"

"I am," said Peter. "I'm paying as little attention as possible!"

"Who can tell me the longest words in the English language?" asked the teacher.

Sandy raised her hand. "Post office!" she said.

"I'm afraid not," smiled the teacher.

"Sure they are," said Sandy. "It has millions of letters!"

Q: What's a wizard's favorite subject?
A: Mathe-magic.

One day, Mrs. Tetsu came home and found young Mei writing on a pad while sitting on the family cat.

"Get off the cat!" Mrs. Tetsu said, with alarm.

"I can't," said Mei. "My homework assignment is to write a paper on my pet!"

Smartie Smedley asked his teacher, "What letter of the alphabet is like New Year's Eve?"

After thinking for a minute, the teacher said, "I have no idea."

Smedley said, "The letter 'R' is like New Year's Eve, because they both come at the end of December."

Q: What's the difference between someone who fishes, and someone who dislikes studying?
A: One baits hooks, the other hates books.

Georgie walked into the house after taking a math exam.

"How did you do?" his mother asked.

"I only got one wrong out of fifty."

"Wow! That's great!"

"No, it isn't," the boy sighed. "I didn't even try to answer the other forty-nine."

The next day, Georgie walked into the house after taking a science test.

"Well?" asked his mother. "Did you have any trouble with the questions."

"Nope," said Georgie. "I only had trouble with the answers."

"If fish cost a dollar a pound," said the math teacher, "how much fish would you get for fifty cents."

"None," said Harold. "I'd get a candy bar."

"Class," said Miss Finch, "who can tell me something that came to the United States from France?"

"French bread," said Vicki.

"And who can tell me something that came to the United States from Italy?"

"Italian dressing," said Rhonda.

"Very good. And who can tell me something that came from Germany?"

"Germs," said Forrest.

"So how did the French test go?" Mrs. Ralston asked her daughter Myrna.

"I got nearly a hundred."

"Fabulous! How close to one hundred did you get?"

"Well . . . I got the zeroes."

The English teacher said, "Listen closely, children, and think hard: Sally sells sea-shells by the seashore. How many "S's" are in that?"

Joy's hand flew up. "There are no "S's" in *that*."

The English teacher continued.
"Who can tell me how to spell 'wrong?' "
Joy said, "R-a-w-n-g."
"That's wrong," said the teacher.
"I know. Isn't that what you wanted?"

The frustrated English teacher said, "Joy, why is it you can never answer my questions correctly?"

"If I could," said Joy, "there wouldn't be any reason for me to come to school!"

The new student, Stupid Steve, walked into class.

"Where are you from, Steve?" the teacher asked.

"Canada, ma'am."
"Oh? What part?"
"All of me, ma'am."

After Stupid Steve sat down, the teacher said, "Who can give me a sentence using the word 'gruesome?' "

Steve raised his hand. "My mom wanted us to eat more vegetables, so she started a garden and grew some."

Later, the teacher asked, "Who can spell the word 'needle?' "

Steve raised his hand. "N-i-e—"

"I'm afraid there's no 'i' in needle."

"No?" said Steve. "Then where does the thread go?"

Still later, the teacher said, "If 'can't' is an abbreviation for 'cannot,' what is 'don't' an abbreviation for?"

Steve shouted, "Doughnut!"

Going nutty from Steve's answers, the teacher called on someone else to answer the next question.

"Jane, can you point to the map and tell me where Hawaii is?"

Jane walked to the map and pointed to the islands.

"Very good," said the teacher. "Now, who can tell me who discovered Hawaii?"

Before she could call on someone else, Steve yelled, "Jane did!"

Gritting her teeth, the teacher asked, "Now, class—which is farther away: Hawaii or the sun?"

Steve called out, "Hawaii! I can see the sun, but I can't see Hawaii."

Because his penmanship was so sloppy, the teacher told Steve to write, "I must write neatly" one hundred times for homework.

The next day, Steve came to class with "I must write neatly" written sixty-two times.

"I thought I told you to write this one hundred times," said the teacher.

"Sorry," said Steve, "but my math is even worse than my writing!"

The history teacher asked, "What is a fortress?"

Bunny raised her hand. "A two-tress plus a two-tress."

Sarah came home after getting her report card.

"Well?" her mother asked. "How did you do?"

"My grades were underwater."

"Underwater? What does that mean?"

"It means they were below C level."

The teacher said to Greedy Ginger, "If you had six cookies, and I asked you for two, how many would you have left?"

Greedy Ginger sneered and answered, "Six."

"What did you learn in school today?" Mrs. Welles asked little Clayton.

"We learned guzzinta."

"What's that?"

"C'mon, ma—you know. Two guzzinta four and four guzzinta eight."

"Have you heard it?" Roger asked his classmates.

"Heard what?"

"My gosh, it's all over the school!"

"*What* is?"

Roger said, "The roof."

The science teacher said to his class, "Now
that we're finished studying the earth, we'll
move on to the moon."

"Wait!" cried Betsy. "Will we be back in
time for dinner?"

The teacher was introducing the new pupil
to her classmates.

"Jeannie, would you tell the class how many
brothers and sisters live in your home?"

"I done got two brothers."

"Now, now," said the teacher, "where's your
grammar?"

"She lives in a different house."

"Roderick," said the math teacher, "if I had ten quarters in my left pocket, ten dimes in my right, and ten nickels in both of my back pockets, what would I have?"

"Heavy pants," Roderick replied.

"Esther," said the English teacher, "can you please define centimeter?"

"Surely," said Esther. "It's when you go to get someone."

"I'm sorry, that's not right—"

"But it is!" Esther protested. "Last week, my big sister came home from college, and my dad and I were *sent to meet her.*"

"Who can tell me why fire engines are red?" the teacher asked.

"I can," said Logical Larry. "They're red because six and six is twelve."

The teacher looked at him. "What does that have to do with it?"

"Well," said Larry, "Six and six is twelve,

twelve inches makes a foot, a foot makes a ruler, a ruler was Queen Elizabeth, the *Queen Elizabeth* sails across the sea, the sea is full of fish, fish have fins, the Finns are located on the Russian border, the Russians are called Reds . . . and fire engines are red because they're always rushin'."

Jamie said, "Ma, I can't go to school today. I don't feel well."

"Where does it hurt?"

Jamie answered, "Whenever I'm in school."

The art teacher handed out crayons and paper and said, "I'd like everyone to draw a ring."

As she walked around the class, she noticed that little Lloyd had drawn a square.

"I thought I told you to draw a ring."

"I did," said Lloyd. "This is a boxing ring."

Martin looked awful when he came home from second grade.

"What's wrong?" asked his mother.

"Well, Ma—first I got punched."

"No!"

"Then I got kicked."

"No!"

"Then I got stabbed, drowned, and clubbed!"

"My goodness!"

"Yes," said Martin, "that was the toughest spelling test I've ever had!"

"How did you do on your report card?" Corwin's mother asked.

"I did the same thing Abraham Lincoln did," said the boy.

"What's that?"

"I went down in history."

The kindergarten teacher asked Hank, "What letter comes after 'A'?"

After thinking for a moment, Hank said, "All the rest of them."

The teacher said to Mr. and Mrs. Wiggins, "I think your daughter is going to grow up to be an astronaut."

"Why do you think that?" asked Mrs. Wiggins.

"Because she just takes up space."

During lunch, the student raised his hand and the teacher came over.

"Mr. Epstein, this bread is hard and stale!"

Breaking off a big piece, the teacher ate it.

"It tastes soft and moist to me."

"It is now," said the student. "I've been chewing it for ten minutes!"

Mrs. Webster said to the second-grade spelling class, "How many days of the week start with the letter 'T'?"

Funny Faye said, "Tuesday, Thursday, today, and tomorrow."

TRANSPORTATION

"Say," said Ollie, "did you hear about the new rule about riding busses?"

"No," said Wally.

"They charge you when you get on . . . *and* when you get off!"

"That's crazy!" said Wally.

"Worse than that," said Ollie, "it's un-fare!"

Q: When is a car not a car?
A: When it turns into a driveway.

Q: What change comes over people when they ride a ferryboat?
A: It makes them cross.

A man came running into the house. "Honey, honey! I just discovered oil!"

"Wonderful!" she said. "Now we can get a new car!"

"We'll have to," the man said. "That's where the oil is coming from."

Q: What's the most loving form of transportation?
A: A boat. It's always hugging the shore.

Q: What kind of vehicle seats two hundred and fifty people and is launched from a bow?
A: An arrow-plane.

Q: What kind of vehicle has a propeller on top and a mountain on the bottom?
A: A hilly-copter.

Mr. Moto walked up to the ticket window at the train station.

"I'd like to buy a roundtrip ticket, please."

"Certainly, sir. Where to?"

"Why, back here, of course!"

A man was walking slowly along the platform to a waiting train.

"Hurry, sir," said the engineer. "This train goes to New York in five minutes."

"Really?" said the man. "Only last month, the trip took an hour."

Q: What's the difference between a railway engineer and a teacher?

A: One minds trains, the other trains minds.

Cabdriver Ogan was checking a fuel tank before taking his cab out, when he saw what he thought was water dripping from a hose. He didn't have his flashlight, so he struck a match. Unfortunately, it wasn't water but fuel. The tank exploded, sending Ogan into orbit.

The next morning, his supervisor sat discussing the tragedy with another driver.

"Ogan was with us for twenty-five years," he said. "I'd have thought that lighting a match near a fuel tank was the *last* thing Ogan would do."

The driver said, "It *was*."

While touring the automobile factory, a senator asked one of the workers, "And how do you make a car top?"

The worker said, "You tep on the brake, tupid!"

Before the plane took off, the flight attendant handed out gum. "This will prevent your ears from popping as we climb."

After the flight, everyone left the plane but one little old man.

"Why are you still here?" the attendant asked.

"You'll have to speak up!" the old man yelled back. "I can't hear very well with this gum in my ears!"

Q: What's the difference between the motto of a boy scout and an auto mechanic?
A: One is "Be Prepared," the other is "Beep Repaired."

The pilot trainer said to his student, "Tomorrow, you'll begin flying solo."
"Really?" said the student. "How low is that?"

Q: What's large, has four wheels, and flies?
A: A garbage truck.

Q: What did the driver say when the bus was caught in an avalanche?
A: "That's just smashing!"

The ship's captain shouted into the radio, "Mayday! We've hit a reef and are sinking!"
"What's your exact position?"
The captain said, "I'm sitting on the bridge!"

Q: How do trains hear?
A: Through their engin-ears.

Q: What is open when it's closed, and closed when it's open?
A: A drawbridge.

Q: What kind of jam can never be spread on bread?
A: A traffic jam.

Q: What kind of motorcycle do comedians ride?
A: A Yamaha-ha-ha.

Q: What about farm animals?
A: They ride Cow-asakis.

Q: What kind of boat leaves a quarter under your pillow?
A: The tooth ferry.

Q: What form of transportation helps you digest your food?
A: A chew-chew train.

VACATIONS

When the Gish family was checking out of the hotel, the man at the reception desk looked at little Jack and said, "So! Are you going to take a plane home?"

"Oh, no," Jack replied. "There'd be no place to keep it."

During the winter vacation, little Timmy came into the house crying.

"Mama!" he wailed. "Joey is only letting me have the sled half the time!"

"Well," said the mother, "it sounds like your brother's being fair—"

"He isn't!" the boy cried. "He gets it going down the hill, and I get it going up!"

While taking a cruise in the Arctic, Mrs. Fein suddenly pointed across the ocean and said, "Look! An iceberg!"

Mr. Fein looked and looked where she was pointing but didn't see a thing.

"Obviously, darling, you have a problem," said Mrs. Fein.

"What problem is that?" he asked.

"Poor ice sight," she replied.

"So," said the father to his kids, "what did you think of the Grand Canyon?"

"It was just gorges," said his son.

While checking into the Florida hotel, the woman from New York said, "We're here for the winter."

"Oh," said the clerk, "then you're going to be terribly disappointed. We don't have winter in Florida!"

Visiting an amusement park on their vacation, the young woman and her husband went on the super-duper roller coaster.

The man was sick as they walked off.

"I want to thank you for taking me on those two rides," he said to his wife.

"Two rides?" she said. "But that was only one."

"No, it was two," he said. "My first and my last."

Q: What did the executioner do on his winter vacation?

A: He stopped slaying and went sleighing.

"I'm frightened," said the passenger to the captain as the cruise ship sailed across the Atlantic. "What if we should sink?"

"Don't worry," said the captain. "We're never more than a few miles from land."

"Really? Which way?"

The captain replied, "Straight down."

Standing at the edge of a cliff, getting ready to go hang gliding for the first time, Jillie asked Millie, the experienced flyer, "Do people often get killed doing this?"

"Don't be silly," said Millie. "You can only get killed once."

The Abrams family was vacationing in Bermuda.

"Dad," said little Charlotte, "why is the seashore always wet?"

Before her father could answer, her brother piped in, "On account of the sea-weed."

"You know, children," said Mr. Abrams, "the last time I was in Bermuda, a lobster crept out of the water and snipped off one of my toes."

"Which one?" asked Charlotte.

"I couldn't tell you that. All lobsters look the same to me."

The Cohen family was driving cross-country, and stopped in a small motel.

"Hi," Mr. Cohen said to the desk clerk. "Would it be okay to stay here for the night?"

The clerk scratched her head. "Sure—but wouldn't you rather have a room instead?"

After checking in, the Cohens went to a local restaurant. A man was playing guitar outside, and the name "Tex" was written across the front of it.

"So," said Mr. Cohen, "your name is Tex."

"That's right."

"Are you from Texas?"

"Nope. I'm from Louisiana."

Mr. Cohen asked, "Then why do you call yourself Tex?"

"Because it's a whole lot better than Louise."

While visiting Atlantic City, the man got on the bus and asked, "Does this bus stop at the ocean?"

"It better," said the driver, "or we're all going to drown."

Q: What state never has a kind word to say about anyone?

A: Rude Island.

After returning from his vacation, Matt said to the other kids in school, "There I was, on horseback, with other horses to my left, a lion in front of me, and an elephant behind me."

"How'd you get out?" asked a friend.

Matt shrugged. "I hopped off the merry-go-round."

Rudy said to Einar, "Did you hear about the man who sold me the Sphinx while I was in the Middle East?"

"Really?" said Einar. "Sounds like Egypt you."

While Rudy was away, he also saw a sign on an Egyptian funeral parlor: "Satisfaction guaranteed, or your mummy back."

Q: Why is it so wet in England?
A: Because kings and queens have been reigning for centuries.

⊘ SIGNET (0451)

MORE BIG LAUGHS

☐ "WHERE'S THE KIDS, HERMAN?" by Jim Unger.　　(157958—$2.25)
☐ "APART FROM A LITTLE DAMPNESS, HERMAN, HOW'S EVERYTHING ELSE?" by Jim Unger.　　(163435—$2.50)
☐ "IN ONE OF YOUR MOODS AGAIN, HERMAN?" by Jim Unger.
　　(134958—$1.95)
☐ "ANY OTHER COMPLAINTS, HERMAN?" by Jim Unger.　(136322—$1.95)
☐ "NOW WHAT ARE YOU UP TO, HERMAN?" by Jim Unger.(156323—$2.50)
☐ "THE CAT'S GOT YOUR TEETH AGAIN, HERMAN" by Jim Unger.
　　(160517—$2.50)
☐ "FEELING RUN DOWN AGAIN, HERMAN?" by Jim Unger. (156374—$2.50)

Prices slightly higher in Canada

Buy them at your local
bookstore or use coupon
on next page for ordering.

SIGNET Reference Books (0451)

☐ **THE NEW AMERICAN DICTIONARY OF GOOD ENGLISH by Normal Lewis.** Improve your language skills. Communicate with complete confidence! If you need a quick review of grammar and usage rules, this comprehensive, easy-to-use reference gives you the skills to read, write and speak correctly. (150236—$4.95)

☐ **THE WRITER'S HOTLINE HANDBOOK by Michael Montgomery and John Stratton.** Developed in response to actual questions asked of the Writer's Hotline service at the University of Arkansas, this authoritative handbook of English language usage gives clear, concise information about basic word choices, punctuation and grammar. (626397—$5.95)

☐ **WRITE FROM THE START Tapping Your Child's Natural Writing Ability, by Donald Graves & Virginia Stuart.** This incisive study, encouraging children to write with their own ideas, also encourages them to learn to read. "A crucial discovery shows parents how they can help children write at home and improve instruction at school."—*The New York Times* (150481—$4.50)

☐ **THE MENTOR GUIDE TO WRITING TERM PAPERS AND REPORTS by William C. Paxson.** A complete guide to the intricacies of grammar, punctuation, vocabulary—all the troublesome aspects of writing a term paper or report. This book provides all the necessary tools for successful writing, from first draft to finished product. (626125—$3.95)

*Prices slightly higher in Canada

Buy them at your local bookstore or use this convenient coupon for ordering.

NEW AMERICAN LIBRARY
P.O. Box 999, Bergenfield, New Jersey 07621

Please send me the books I have checked above. I am enclosing $_____ (please add $1.00 to this order to cover postage and handling). Send check or money order—no cash or C.O.D.'s. Prices and numbers are subject to change without notice.

Name_____

Address_____

City _____ State _____ Zip Code _____

Allow 4-6 weeks for delivery.
This offer, prices and numbers are subject to change without notice.

Ⓢ **SIGNET** Ⓜ **MENTOR**

FOR YOUR REFERENCE SHELF

(0451)

☐ **NEW AMERICAN DESK ENCYLCOPEDIA.** The comprehensive, one-volume paperback guide that combines information on all major fields of knowledge with up-to-date coverage of the contemporary world scene. With over 14,000 entries. Perfect for home, school, and office.   (158180—$6.95)

☐ **SLANG AND EUPHEMISM by Richard A. Spears.** Abridged. From slang terminology describing various bodily functions and sexual acts to the centuries-old cant of thieves and prostitutes to the language of the modern drug culture, here are 13,500 entries and 30,000 definitions of all the words and expressions so carefully omitted from standard dictionaries and polite conversation.   (165543—$5.95)

☐ **THE LIVELY ART OF WRITING by Lucile Vaughan Payne.** An essential guide to one of today's most necessary skills. It illumines the uses—and misuses—of words, sentences, paragraphs, and themes, and provides expertly designed exercises to insure thorough understanding.   (627121—$4.50)

☐ **THE BASIC BOOK OF SYNONYMS AND ANTONYMS by Laurence Urdang.** Expand your vocabulary while adding variety to your writing with thousands of the most commonly used words in the English language. Alphabetically arranged for quick and easy use, this indispensable guide includes sample sentences for each word.   (161947—$4.95)

Prices slightly higher in Canada

Buy them at your local

bookstore or use coupon

on next page for ordering.

⊕ MENTOR ⊘ **SIGNET**

WORDLY WISE

(0451)

☐ **ALL ABOUT WORDS by Maxwell Numberg and Morris Rosenblum.** Two language experts call on history, folklore, and anecdotes to explain the origin, development, and meaning of words. (625986—$4.95)

☐ **INSTANT WORD POWER by Norman Lewis.** A fast, effective way to build a rich and dynamic vocabulary. Entertaining exercises and challenging self-tests enable the student to master hundreds of new words and polish spelling and grammar skills. (166477—$5.95)

☐ **MASTERING SPEED READING by Norman C. Maberly.** Basic steps and drills with illustrations, charts and tests provide self-instruction in speed reading. (166442—$4.95)

Prices slightly higher in Canada

Buy them at your local bookstore or use this convenient coupon for ordering.

NEW AMERICAN LIBRARY
P.O. Box 999, Bergenfield, New Jersey 07621

Please send me the books I have checked above. I am enclosing $_____
(please add $1.00 to this order to cover postage and handling). Send check or money order—no cash or C.O.D.'s. Prices and numbers are subject to change without notice.

Name_____

Address_____

City _____ State _____ Zip Code _____
Allow 4-6 weeks for delivery.
This offer, prices and numbers are subject to change without notice.

There's an epidemic with 27 million victims. And no visible symptoms.

It's an epidemic of people who can't read.

Believe it or not, 27 million Americans are functionally illiterate, about one adult in five.

The solution to this problem is you... when you join the fight against illiteracy. So call the Coalition for Literacy at toll-free 1-800-228-8813 and volunteer.

Volunteer Against Illiteracy. The only degree you need is a degree of caring.

THIS AD PRODUCED BY MARTIN LITHOGRAPHERS
A MARTIN COMMUNICATIONS COMPANY